Taking Notice

Taking Notice

Poems
by
Patricia McNair

Mayapple Press, 2007

Published by Mayapple Press
408 N. Lincoln St.
Bay City, MI 48708
www.mayapplepress.com

ISBN 978-0932412-560

"In the Forest" and "Dawn, Dec. 15, 2002" first appeared in *Jihad bil Qalam, "To Strive by Means of the Pen," A TCAP Anti-War Anthology,* edited by Marc Beaudin.

Photographs by Patricia McNair.

Book designed and typeset by Judith Kerman in Adobe Caslon Pro with Alliance titles.

In Memoriam, Patricia McNair
1927-2007

Contents

Pleasing My Mother	3
Pa-paw's Seasons	4
That Rooster	5
Watching	6
Hoping for a Smoother Ride	7
One of Those Sundays	8
Timeline	9
Taking the Train 1946	11
Hanging Clothes	12
Pebbles I	13
Creature	14
Dis-ease	15
Poem of a Double Life	16
Collections	17
New Beginning	18
A Different Autumn	19
Sorting Out	20
Choosing a New Name	21
Pebbles II	22
Rescue Effort	23
Toys	24
Dawn, Dec. 15, 2002	25
Morning Mystery	26
Tour Group Visits	27
Dawn	28
Working Together	29
Menace	30
The Dance	31
Mushrooms in October	32
Surprise	33
Reading the Signs	34
A Parched Summer	35
Late August	36
Pebbles III	37
"What Big Ears You Have, Grandma!"	38
Six a.m. Along Highway 52	39
A Craving	40
Beware	41
Wondering	42

Misreading the Signs	43
A Harvest of Diamonds	44
A Tangle . . .	45
Trying To Get It Right	46
Request	47
In the Forest	48
Radiation	49
A Bad Feather Day	52
In My Next Life	53
Immortality	54
Requiem	55
Poets Gather	56

Pleasing My Mother

(For Ramona Herron Cadenhead, 1907-1968)

I never thought of it this way before.
Trying to please my mother by
planting nasturtiums over and over . . .
beginning in the hard clay of a Lansing yard,
our first home as young married students,
where the landlady charged extra
to park a car under her only tree.

Then in Iowa's black dirt,
too rich for such a common plant,
or was I too busy with a new baby
and no washing machine? Next in Okemos,
where the Michigan clay scraped my knuckles,
and the seeds never took hold.
I tried another time in the sandy soil
of South Bend, and a few years later
under a window in a suburb of Chicago.

This is the memory that kept me strewing seeds:
At dusk my mother would send me out
to gather a bouquet for the dinner table.
I enjoyed snapping those crisp stems,
admiring the combination of yellow and orange.
She never taught me the rules of planting and caring,
only to harvest, like a small princess sent out
in a fresh frock, with an oval basket over her arm,
to gather blossoms the gardener had raised

I tried again just this year, in Saginaw,
where the valley earth seems to be just right—
planted two packets of seeds
and left town for awhile.
My mother would have been one hundred,
had she lived. She would be pleased
with this splash of orange and yellow
next to my patio, and the small vase
of blossoms beside my chair.

Pa-paw's Seasons

(Robert Walton Cadenhead, Sr. 1867-1945)

When I sat beside him on the porch swing, both of us trying to be cool in shorts those hot Oklahoma days, his knees were great feverish knobs. When his hands grasped his smooth brown cane I saw his knuckles were swollen and red. His shoulders were wide, his back remained straight, although he could no longer work in our neighborhood grocery store. Asthma rattled in his chest, and he kept a large white handkerchief constantly at hand. This was Pa-paw in summer.

Winter Sundays found him in his arm chair beside the great stone fireplace at the farm, a shawl over his shoulders, his cane leaning against his legs. The crackling fire warmed his knees and knuckles, easing the pain. One Sunday I brought the Bible and opened it on his lap. "Find the twenty-third Psalm," I directed. "I'll read it to you." Then, keeping my eyes on the page, I recited the Psalm, wanting desperately to be able to read at age four. I could tell he was proud that I could read. This was Pa-paw in winter.

That Rooster

(Earliest Memory)

The yard seems vast, the house far away.
A ladder lies flat across the grass
between me and the house, an obstacle
for unsteady legs of a two-year old
trying to reach one end,
then the other.
No matter how I hurry the rooster is there,
on the other side of the ladder,
blocking my way with awful flapping wings,
sharp beak thrust forward,
mean eyes glaring. Finally my mother
rushes out, gathers me to safety.

I was told later
that my twin brother trailed behind her
calling, "Don't let that rooster get my baby!"
Then my dad left the store, briefly,
and wrung that rooster's neck,
then and there!

Watching

The chasing of the chickens
inside the pens, the desperate clucking,
the suspicious flapping of wings,
the whole general uproar.

The carrying to the chopping stump,
held upside down by its ankles,
wings still flapping.

The head on the block, beak open,
eyes wild, wings flapping.
The neck under the single blow of the ax,

the headless body jerking, flopping
in the sparse grass and dry soil,
wings flapping yet.

The rough clasping of the ankles again,
the now-still body held above the bucket
of boiling water for the quick dunk
to scald the feathers loose,
the wings dangling, dripping.

The quick habit-honed plucking of feathers,
the slick white fowl ready
to be gutted, feet cut off, wings folded.
The hens ready to roast,

the fryers separated into parts
with the sharp knife, practice made perfect
by my grandmother and mother;
a task I refused to learn,
always buying pre-cut chickens
in these sixty years since.

Hoping for a Smoother Ride

My brother and I are thirteen, it is January of 1940. My parents admire a '37 Chevy sedan, almost new, a good buy, and beautiful in the fresh snow: tomato-red. In it they feel beautiful, almost as if they had money.

Things will be better now. They feel this in their hearts. By next summer it will rain, grass will grow in the yards again, the neighbors will find jobs and eat better and get their teeth fixed. Next summer Hitler will stop taking countries.

Our dad is worried about the "balloon payment" due in eighteen months. My twin brother and I make a secret pact to save half our allowance of fifty cents a week to help pay for our new car. In eighteen months we will surprise our dad with thirty-nine dollars, half the amount of that last payment.

One of Those Sundays

My twin brother and our cousin, four years older,
head across the back yard and down the lane
to the rusting body of a model T
in the weeds. I tag along.
It's Sunday, with the family
gathered at my uncle's farm.
Grandparents and aunts, only two cousins.
The other girl, in her teens, doesn't play
with eight-year olds.

Mid-Depression, no rain for five years,
the hard dirt lane lined with dusty weeds.
I have no memory of green grass,
of squishing mud between my toes
in a summer rain
I settle with the boys in the old car,
our favorite playhouse at the farm.

We talk awhile and then, in silence,
my cousin opens his pants, pulls out
a whitish grub, his eyes watching me
as I watch. I leave,
walk back to the farm house, knowing
boys have a weapon to use against us,
a way to say we don't want you around.

Timeline

In the cool of morning
the road fronting our store
beckoned me — two blocks long, the spine
of our neighborhood. Houses crouched
among vacant lots, our grocery
the only business. We lived at the rear.

In the summer heat
we put footprints in the soft black tar
of the road, though it burned bare feet,
kept us dancing along, or seeking
the dusty path beside it. I'd cross
to the ditch on the other side,
to gather seeds to put in mud pies.

Children walked this road
to buy candy at our store. Lucky kids . . .
our mother refused us candy and pop.
In summer we begged for chunks of ice
from the ice man's dripping truck,
ran out when we heard the bell
of the Good Humor Man. A stick
of orange sherbet covered with chocolate
was my choice.

On this road, day after day, my mother carried
lunch on a tray to an ill neighbor.
Trotting beside her, I clutched
a tiny vase of fresh flowers. Up and down
this road I walked and ran and bicycled,
watched "Defense Houses" being built
during World War II, and envied
my brother's self-assurance, greeting
new neighbors as they unloaded their trucks.

My winter wedding day
was so cold our car refused to start.
Ready to go to the church, I stood on this road

in my white satin wedding dress watching
my dad and brother push the car. Would it start?
I could see them moving slowly
further and further away . . . the black road
trailing behind them.

Taking the Train 1946

I wasn't nervous about the dress fitting,
the rehearsal, the wedding,
my Dad giving me away,
the reception, the clutch of relatives.
The night in a Tulsa hotel
didn't fill me with trepidation.
But a train berth from Tulsa
to Lansing, Michigan seemed scary.
Could we share it? I asked. And we did.

"Oh dear, you have to go through
that Sinful City, Chicago,"
my grandmother had exclaimed.
Not only Chicago, but first Kansas City,
famous for gangsters and jazz,
and crossing the Mississippi!
I had never traveled east of Oklahoma.

The landscape changing
to the rhythm of wheels on rails,
the coming of night,
darkness sprinkled with tiny lights
like low stars. As promised,
the car was left in Lansing at midnight,
disconnected from the train
that sped on to Canada while we slept.

At eight a.m., hand in hand,
we stepped
down to the platform
into our new life.

Hanging Clothes

While I hang my grandsons' shirts on the line
the ashen clouds gather in the west.
The tree house, anchored on two shagbark
hickories and two maples,
creaks in the wind.
The rhythmic sound comforts.
It will surely sing boys to sleep
wrapped in their bed rolls,
as a cradle might soothe baby Caitlin
with a soft chirr, and as the swing
hung from an oak branch
once delighted their dad.

Pebbles I

Summer

The grass crunches
but I keep
the flowers watered.

Autumn

Leaves,
hanging on,
smiling colors.

Winter

Skies scare us,
oh, dear,
we're in for it!

Spring

Listen—
stems rising,
still out of sight.

Creature

Something is eating my house. It
gnaws at the front door frame. Perhaps
it is one of our squirrels who scamper
up and down the tall oaks and maples,
make forays to the bird feeder, chase
each other in a game of hide and seek
around the tree trunks. Perhaps it
is a nocturnal animal who wakes
stretching as the light leaves the sky,
its large eyes able to see the way to the porch
at midnight, its teeth sharp and vicious.
It gradually strips away the wood
until the hole could hide
a folder of credit cards,
a chain of keys, or a love letter . . .

The experts cemented the hole,
painted it over. I sighed in relief.
Complacency set in. Then one night,
startled awake, I know the creature
is once again at my door,
shredding the wood,
chipping the paint . . .

Dis-ease

At first it seemed
innocent. Neither
meant real harm, just
enchanted with possibility.
Why didn't I see
the brick loosened,
mortar sifting
in crumbs, here,
and here, and here,
like Gretel's
dropped bread.

I feel alarm
in my house.
Yesterday I noticed
another brick had been
edged loose.
Deterioration becoming
obvious in the back,
while in the front
still hidden.

I am uneasy
leaving.
Returning,
what will I find?
Today a wall
shifted.
And now, night
is approaching.

Poem of a Double Life

Rushing out on errands . . .
bank, market, cleaners,
fill the car with gas,
get home to do laundry.
My mind churning, I drive
past my turn. Is he
meeting her for lunch,
this is her day off . . .
Fresh flowers on the table,
I bought them myself, matching
the candles. The setting festive,
though mood isn't.
He insisted, last Saturday, that
I get the prescriptions now,
right now. I gave him two hours
to talk on the phone in private.
I'm behind in everything, not days,
but weeks. I meet only absolute
deadlines. Letters, shopping, writing:
clutter builds, guilt nags.
Has no one noticed this
enchantment? Secret code looks,
the furtive hand, the private
joke . . . so blatant, I see it all.
I call friends, talk of nothing. Go to
matinees, forget meetings, neglect
the cleaning. Fantasy flames. I pick up
job applications . . . don't fill them out.
He declares he loves me, she
has nothing to do with our love,
our life. Perhaps he can tame it,
but will not give her up!
I love him. Will I lose him? Can we
work it out? Still, I feel myself
changing. I finger the valentines
in the rack. They mock me.

Collections

Sometimes we shake out of a pail
a scattering of colored stones,
the click against each other.
Or tiny buttons in a flat Lucky Strike box,
a rustle against the metal.

Then there is the boy's denim bag
of marbles, all bright colors.
My mother's jewelry box,
a jumble of beads
glittering in the light . . .

So it was I toyed with the lid
of the small brass box on the end table.
Talking with my husband,
not even thinking about the contents,
I flipped the lid back and forth,

enjoying the small smack
of metal against metal, until
I turned toward it,
catching a glimpse—
dozens of tiny faces
cut from snapshots,
face after face . . . all the same,
all the same woman's face.
And not my face.

New Beginning

Don't tell me how a spartan attitude
would help on a day like this.
I packed every carton
and know the work it will take
to fit all of it into this small space.
This unloading of the van is sad
for me to watch. How to arrange
this furniture in my new place?

I was hot and tired when he strolled
up the walk. How dare he show his face,
so brown from days spent at the shore,
while I had pulled painfully
at my roots, and not by choice.

I threatened him with mayhem,
raged and swore. And I tell you now,
when this unpacking is all finished, both
anger and love will have diminished.

A Different Autumn

I am dazzled by this color,
these golden trees,
every shade and hue of yellow
to mustard to orange.
I turn a corner and am stunned
by a wealth of reds,
the richness of burgundy.
A few green branches
clinging to summer.

Was it just last year
I saw autumn
approach in brown,
plain as a monk's robe,
dragging sadly toward winter?
Was that just a year ago?

Sorting Out

He packed and fled,
leaving bits of his history behind:
two paintings from Paris
which never interested me,
though they once hung over our bed,
a set of classics bound in small volumes
from his favorite aunt's library,
a framed picture of his grandmother,
tall and regal in a white dress,
and a photograph of his grandson at twelve.

I've set them aside, debating with myself
about disposal.
It has been three years now.
My anger has mellowed,
but my finances have decreased
. . . there would be the postage . . .
Do I succumb to my sentimental nature
and send them . . .?

Oh, to hell with it!
I'll drop them in the Goodwill box.

Choosing a New Name

Our names are part of our wholeness.
Madeleine L'Engle

Deceit, betrayal, divorce.
I give myself a new name,
send out announcements
as if a birth has occurred,
print it across my life
like a stamp on a passport
when entering a different country.
I decide I'll stay.
I like it here.

Pebbles II

For Shirley

Tomatoes cluster on every branch,
her garden as profuse
as her seventy years of giving.

August

Roses, asters, geraniums, phlox,
shades of pinks and purples.
Behold this treasure!

Rescue Effort

This is the last stand of Queen Anne's Lace
in the subdivision. It grows at the curb
surrounded on three sides by baked clay
from the excavation for a house.
I carry a small bucket, trowel and clippers,
planning to rescue this clump of Lace
from the lawn people.

I lift a few clods the size of baseballs,
expose pale yellow stems twisting across
eight inches between the healthy plant
and the still buried roots. The remaining
clay is in chunks too large to push aside.
I scrabble with my trowel
and decide I must wait for rain.
Failure reminds me of hundreds,
who cannot wait,
desperately lifting beams, moving bricks
and boards, digging to reach victims.

I give up stabbing at the hard earth,
clip off a bouquet to carry home.
My mind is on Fallujah and Baghdad,
Palestine and Israel, Spain and New York City.
I arrange the blossoms in a green glass vase,
notice the sky clouding over and think how
"waiting" is a luxury in this sad world.

Toys

Northbound, I am two cars back, waiting
to turn left. A moving van, southbound,
approaching properly through the intersection,
is hit by a green sports car,
which flies to shambles.
Not only a crushed front but suddenly
disjointed, as if all its body parts
came unglued.

The van pulls to a stop, the driver amazed,
as though stung by a bee that falls dead.
The rest of us move on. I heard a bang,
saw the sports car fall apart

like the plastic crash-mobiles my sons
delighted in years ago. The cars, aimed
at each other or at a wall, given a push,
would simply fly apart at impact . . .
hood, roof, doors, chassis, trunk . . . to be
snapped back together for another go.

Dawn, Dec. 15, 2002

*(While reading **Fuel** by Naomi Shihab Nye)*

Seven forty-five, black branches appear
against a night-blue sky.
I am reading poetry by Naomi Shihab Nye.
She writes of war in Palestine,
an Iraqi woman feeding her ducks
in America, saddened by war
between her two countries.

As dawn slowly reveals my yard,
the neighbor's swing set, the bird bath,
I read more poems. This writer
is half American, half Middle Eastern.
There is never despair in her words
only truth of how women feel
when food is scarce, bombs shock,
no one has parties any more.

The sky becomes a pale blue,
winter grass shows dull green,
the clock ticks. It's Sunday morning.
These poems were published in 1998.
How many days have dawned since then?
How many women still suffer in the Middle East?
Moment by moment the light changes . . .

Morning Mystery

In the morning sun and touched
by a slight breeze,
white-caps move on a sea of grass—
miniature ocean waves.
I walk closer . . . closer.
Tiny cobwebs grace the back yard.
Each web, nickle-size, barely touches
the tips of grass blades.
A single thread connects the webs
in sparkling scallops.
It appears a delicate silvery crust.
The manna must have looked like this!

Tour Group Visits

The small spruce is aquiver with birds.
They hide inside, flutter, come out,
peck at the branches, drop to the grass.

Like a small beige cloud they fly to the garden.
I count seven sitting on the edge
of the birdbath, side by side in a circle,
shouldering one another, constantly
changing places, playing musical chairs.
They sip the water, their heads going
up and down like piano keys.
A few venture a bath, flapping, splashing.

Still moving as a group, they explore
the patio, hop up onto the large stone,
test the birch logs. One spies
the geranium above its head,
hops up to take a closer look.

I must have missed the signal, but . . .
there they go . . . off together
through this July sunshine.

Dawn

Every tree branch piled with snow.
The rising sun spreading a glow
of pink across the sky
from east to west behind
and high above all this white.

Working Together

Pieces of string,
grayed by dust and weather,
taken from last year's
garden stakes
and cut into shorter lengths,
now hang on a small spruce
and drape haphazardly
on spiked driftwood.

A female finch
picks at strands with her beak
like a woman fingering yarn
for her next project.
Choosing, she flies away,
string trailing.

Menace

A groundhog runs across my neighbor's yard
hustling under the deck.
He sets off alarms in my mind
of friends who have waged war
on groundhogs because
of collateral damage.
I imagine the groundhog digging holes
under the deck, just as he must
have tunneled under the fence,
his fat body too big to go through.
He reminds me of a crouched sniper
scurrying across an open area,
darting into a doorway.

The groundhog is the enemy in these parts.
Yet, he is doing exactly what
he was created to do,
or perhaps has evolved to do.
Maybe he is a she,
an even more dangerous threat,
reproduction being what it is.
And what of the sniper,
shooting at random
or with deadly intent . . .
was this what he was made for?
Or has the killer evolved
out of collateral damage
to his own innocent life?

Are groundhogs and snipers
proliferating in our
complex and speeding country?

The Dance

A pair of purple finches
swoop in for a sip of water.
He in his red waistcoat,
　　　new and bright.
She, leading their flight,
perches on the splintered branch
　　　of driftwood.
They dance into the sky,
rising, dipping,
waving the banner of spring
　　　across the morning.

Mushrooms in October

They wait beside the driveway,
near the garage where the shade
deepens all day.
The father trying to reach twin toddlers
who are engrossed in a red leaf
and perilously close to the pavement.
A little behind him the family clusters—
mother, three children, a baby
wrapped tightly against the dampness.
All have the same gold-brown hair,
all wear rough white robes,
their post legs anchoring them.
No flights of fancy for these spirits
except in my mind.

Surprise

Escaping the sprinkler the baby rabbit
speeds out of the flower bed,
            trips,
turns a small furry somersault,
races into the next yard,
soothes his beating heart by freezing,
as though playing Statues.

Reading the Signs

Suppose I had not read a newspaper
nor heard a radio.
Suppose I had been away a month.
What would I know from these signs:
paths of crushed grass,
bright balloons hanging from towering trees,
plastic fencing here and there,
dumpsters overflowing to the delight of gulls.
I would notice these signs and know
a mighty throng had gathered here.

And what of more subtle signs?
That heron flies over as I water my garden,
your favorite mock orange
blooms out of season,
the weed you used for dried arrangements
appears for the first time
among my flowers,
These signs tell me your spirit
is abroad, comes near . . .
an invisible finger touches my lips . . .
shh . . . don't tell.

A Parched Summer

In my neighbor's yard, gone brown,
the clump of Queen Anne's Lace
stands green and pretty.
I covet this wild flower,
even as my neighbor growls,
"I'm gonna cut down that damn weed!"
And he did.

Late August

Smoke rises from our breakfast beach fire,
travels out over the jeweled lake.
Shades of blue, horizontal lines
where color fades or brightens.
The green of distant tree-covered hills
greyed by fog.
This largess will fire winter dreams.

Pebbles III

1.

My small flower bed
abounds in color,
crowded but happy.

2.

Three back yards away
he bounds and plays.
I call him "The Happy Dog."

3.

The young men next door
remind me of my grandsons,
handsome, sweet, lazy.

4.

We relax in lawn chairs,
in a surround of large trees.
Music spreads across the park.

"What Big Ears You Have, Grandma!"

Ever since I read
that our ears never stop growing
mine haven't.
Some women focus on their hips
or waist, or breasts,
but I worry morning, noon, and eve
about my ears, forget the rest.
Will they really grow ALL my life?
Shoulder length perhaps?
I hear them growing, growing
during the night,
am tempted to measure, but resist
and push away the fear as I recall . . .
"The better to hear you with, my dear!"

Six a.m. Along Highway 52

My friend grew up
on an Iowa farm—
how she enjoyed this journey

between our towns,
when she could
still find her way.

Blue sky streaked with gray,
early sun flaring
from behind clouds.

Mist rises, as though
all the valleys were smoldering.
Ponds steam.

Though touched with frost, the fields
are furrows of new green,
like pin stripes in a man's suit.

Last year's corn stubble
reflects the sun,
coins scattered across the field.

She would have commented
on all this beauty,
while zipping past farmland.

When I arrive we will have
breakfast on her porch.
Will she remember who I am?

A Craving

It's been a long time since I've been ill,
and I am hankering for a sick day.
Nothing serious, mind you,
but a day or two when weakness
sends me to the couch to linger
wan and listless.
Someone must come in
to fetch a cool cloth for my fevered brow,
a bowl of hot soup, a cup of herbal tea,
and I will read and read and read.
I'll start at the top of that stack
of books under the t.v.,
or that stack over there . . . or the other
beside the stereo. Oh dear, I am feeling faint
just making the decision.
Perhaps it could be managed without the fever.

Beware

(In the voice of a grandson)

Grandma is a poetry pusher
and she belongs to a gang.
It was years before I realized
what a menace she is.
A book every birthday, *Pat the Bunny*
through *Winnie-the-Pooh*,
on to *Tom Sawyer* and *Treasure Island.*
Then, she slipped it in . . .
Poems to Read to Your Girlfriend.

Visiting her, I noticed how she deals.
The innocence of a coffee shop,
non-fat muffins with de-caf.
The gang had their bags with them,
furtively pulling out a bit of the drug.
They were addicted for sure.
Taking turns, reading aloud,
sighing or laughing.
I could see they knew a good thing.

Maybe every third birthday,
the illicit book of poetry.
Some I ignored, left on the shelf,
tried not to fall for it all.
The year Billy Collins appeared . . .
well, I was hooked.
Maybe this year,
Garrison Keillor's *Good Poems*,
'cause I'm ready for the next hit.

Wondering

What is fog but clouds
come down to surround us,
spreading among the trees.
All is hidden.
When we venture into fog it is gone,
yet always before us
and still behind us. Stretched
to gossamer thinness, it baffles
or delights us, brings mystery to our day.
What is fog but clouds gone astray.

Misreading the Signs

I should have known,
even though the calendar says spring,
even though Easter approaches,
even though we've not had snow for a month.
I should have known.

I rejoiced in the warmth of sunshine,
watched the wings' rhythmic flap
of geese returning northward,
eased into a porch chair
in contentment and certainty.

I should have known
not to loiter in the warm breeze
under a promising sky.
There were signs I forgot to read,
his reassurances so glibly spoken,
her friendship slightly brittle, too bright.

I should have gathered my supplies
and started on this
cold and lonely journey.

A Harvest of Diamonds

The lawn is scattered with diamonds
sparkling in the morning sun.
How frustrating it would be
if one were searching this day
for the diamond ring
slung out into the dark grass last night
in a fit of anger.
It is a good thing the two of them
took flashlight in hand, forgetting
their argument, and searched
on their knees inch after inch
for two hours . . . The diamonds
on the grass sparkle before me
bringing this memory from years ago.
And how the two of them laughed
when recalling that anger-laden night.

A Tangle . . .

The long-
stemmed
cosmos
fell over
in the
dense rain.
I gathered
the loose
bundle
of feathery
leaves,
drooping
blossoms,
all shades
of pink.
Put
in a jug
of water
they were
still
distraught,
hardly
knew
where
to turn
their
glowing
faces.

Trying To Get It Right

Bought a bird bath for the patio.
It is a cement bowl
so heavy I can't lift it,
looking for all the world
like a curled-up cat:
ears, eyes, whiskers, and a smug
expression—its tail curled around.
We bought it to celebrate
our twenty years of marriage.

I've learned a lot about bird baths
with this cat. No, she doesn't scare
the birds away. They come to get drinks,
as do the squirrels. But when it comes
to bathing . . . it is just that . . .
she is too deep for the small birds,
too small for the larger birds. With their
longer legs they can touch bottom,
but their wings scrape the sides.
With no pedestal it is too close
to the ground for relaxed bathing,
constant vigilance required.

And you know what?
The marriage wasn't so great either!

Request

With open palm touch my hair:
admire the grey.

Learn to love these wrinkles,
they're here to stay.

This body won't thin-down,
though I pray.

Even you may sometimes look
the other way.

Just don't stray. OK?

In the Forest

The voice of the Lord makes the oaks to whirl,
and strips the forests bare,
and in his temple all cry, "Glory!"
Psalm 29, Verse 9

Through the forest of oaks and maples,
of hickory and walnut, comes a voice,
so strong a voice the oaks whirl
and leaves rush off the trees,
nuts rattle to the earth,
a rabbit quivers under a pile of brush.

The Lord speaks . . . more leaves fly.
"I am here,"
        "Pay attention,"
                "Changes are needed,"
                        "Love one another,"
or only, "Winter is coming."

Perhaps each of us, standing in the forest,
holding coats close around us,
watching the oaks twist and whirl,
will hear a unique message.
Something we need to know,
that may change our direction,
show us a path swept clean by that voice.

Maybe it will be simple:
        "Be grateful."
And, perhaps, in this forest,
we will all cry, "Peace!"

Radiation

I. Respite

The balloon messaging "Get Well"
sways near the ceiling, and I have
two days at home to do as I please,
grateful not to spend from 11:12 to 11:25
on the hard table watching the great white arm
with its Cyclops eye slowly circle my body,
beaming radiation I cannot see or feel.
Its whirring and high-pitched whine informs.

Overnight snow weighs down
the evergreen,
morning sun casts long shadows,
crows call across high branches.
Three crystals, suspended on the window,
send colored lights about the room
moving as the heat comes on.

II. A Shadow

The table is hard, a glass top actually,
and I am once again flat on my back,
unmoving as the radiation begins . . .
Above me a huge photograph,
five ceiling panels long,
glares with its bright colors back-lighted.
A small stream, tree trunks,
beds of red and yellow tulips, grass
and daffodils. All the colors pure primary,
meant to offer nature's beauty as hope.
At least I think that is the purpose.
Someone must have suggested:
"This needs some movement in it,
a fish leaping out of the stream perhaps."
And it was added.
Each day I've studied that image, so out of place,
a "fish out of water." Like a black construction paper
fish pasted quickly on the photograph,
missing the mark, appearing to be leaping
out of a tulip. It is a dark shadow
on an ordinary photo,
a cancer marring an x-ray.

III. Reluctance

Is this going to be like summer camp?
This daily gathering with other women,
with nurses and technicians,
strangers sharing a similar purpose,
becoming friends, greeting, chatting, caring . . .
until finally that last day comes.
This routine, this comfort zone, ending.
Goodbyes are made reluctantly,
sad even for that small girl
who hadn't wanted to go to camp
in the first place.

A Bad Feather Day

While on the phone with the doctor,
I watch the young robin
who has swooped in
for his morning bath. He hops
into the water, dunks his head,
flaps about.

Onto the rim of the bird bath,
shaking off the water,
his feathers puffed. Then,
into the water again. The same routine.
After his third bath he is thoroughly
askew.

I hang up the phone,
feeling as disheveled as he.
Tests again, and more treatment
for the cancer we thought we'd beaten.
Another wait between appointments . . .
I want to plunge in now,
rid my body of this invasion,
then hop up on the rim of my days,
shake it all off,
fly back into my real life.

In My Next Life

In my next life
I shall sing
with a low melting voice,
not in musicals and concerts,
not even in a church choir.
You will hear my song from the pew.
I will sing with friends around
a piano. And I shall sing when driving,
as did my mother and dad
from the front seat of our old Chevy,
in perfect harmony, in love with each other,
while I pretended sleep.

And I shall dance.
not in perfect step, in a perfect line,
on a stage with footlights;
not in flowing organza around a ballroom.
But through a meadow,
or just across my back yard
in the moonlight,
naked,
as my cousin did when I was twelve.

Immortality

The sky is clear and pale.
Is heaven really up there?
Ancient people believed
in levels of the world.
Heaven, earth, hell.
I think hell is here on earth;
we make it ourselves.
What of heaven? I don't know.

Yet, I believe in immortality.
The spirits of the dead surround us.
Sometimes we take notice.
There, this February morning
with snow melted off the garden,
is the very spirit of my mother
speaking to me
from the first green shoots of the daffodils.

Requiem

(For Mardy Oeming)

The ashen sky tears open,
the sun reaches through,
a small black hawthorn glistens.
Birds explode
from a distant oak,
rise, wheel, approach, turn,
then loop away into the far sky,
settling again
in the huge tree.
The clouds stitch closed.

The sun slips through again,
shines on wet bare branches
as long clouds slide open.
The birds rise in a cluster,
fly nearer,
descend and swerve,
sweep past, wings dipping.

Again and again this music.

Poets Gather

to share their work.
"I'm writing a series
about the north woods," one explains.
We enter the forest with him,
imagine huge trees, twisted roots.
I read about daffodils my mother grew.
She loved the yellow spring blooms,
celebrated them with bouquets,
planned dinners to match their color.

Another poet shares a series
he calls, "Conversations Overheard,"
brings people alive to us,
eavesdropping served up in accents,
whispers, laughter, tears.
I share my memory of being ill as a child,
my mother caring for me with trays of food,
a cool hand on my forehead, extra pillows.

The evening is drawing to a close,
wine glasses empty, shoes off, backs slouched.
A woman reads another of her series
about gardening: the work of it,
the joy of it, early sprouts most of us,
walking past, would never notice.
When I read again
it comes to me . . .
I've been writing a series about my mother.
And why not,
she pulled me to poetry
reading aloud in her quiet voice.

Other recent titles from Mayapple Press:

James Owens, *Frost Lights a Thin Flame*, 2007
Paper, 48 pp, $13.95 plus s&h
ISBN 978-0932412-553
Chris Green, *The Sky Over Walgreens*, 2007
Paper, 74 pp, $14.95 plus s&h
ISBN 978-0932412-546
Mariela Griffor, *HOUSE*, 2007
Paper, 50 pp, $14.95 plus s&h
ISBN 978-0932412-539
John Repp, *Fever,* 2007
Paper, 36 pp, $11.95 plus s&h
ISBN 978-0932412-522
Kathryn Kirkpatrick, *Out of the Garden*, 2007
Paper, 80 pp, $14.95 plus s&h
ISBN 978-0932412-515
Gerry LaFemina, *The Book of Clown Baby/Figures from the Big Time Circus Book,* 2007
Paper, 60 pp, $14.95 plus s&h
ISBN 978-0932412-508
Nancy Botkin, *Parts That Were Once Whole*, 2007
Paper, 72 pp, $14.95 plus s&h
ISBN 978-0932412-492
David Lunde, *Instead,* 2007
Paper, 72 pp, $14.95 plus s&h
ISBN 978-0932412-485
Zilka Joseph, *Lands I Live In*, 2007
Paper, 42 pp, $12.95 plus s&h
ISBN 978-0932412-478
Johanny Vásquez Paz, *Poemas Callejeros/Streetwise Poems*, 2007
Paper, 74 pp, $14.95 plus s&h
ISBN 978-0932412-461
Larry Levy, *I Would Stay Forever If I Could and New Poems,* 2007
Paper, 60 pp, $12.95 plus s&h
ISBN 0-932412-45-9
Christine Hamm, *The Transparent Dinner*, 2006
Paper, 90 pp, $15.95 plus s&h
ISBN 0-932412-44-0

For a complete catalog of Mayapple Press publications, please visit our website at *www.mayapplepress.com.* Books can be ordered direct from our website with secure on-line payment using PayPal, or by mail (check or money order). Or order through your local bookseller.